Chasing Sunsets

Seeking Peace through Prayer

SHANNON LEIGH

ISBN 978-1-63814-141-9 (Paperback)
ISBN 978-1-63814-142-6 (Digital)

All scriptures, unless otherwise stated, are taken from the New International Version of the Holy Bible.

Covenant Books, Inc.
11661 Hwy 707
Murrells Inlet, SC 29576
www.covenantbooks.com

You will seek me and find me when you seek me with all your heart.
—Jeremiah 29:13

How does a sunset make you feel? Are you a sunset chaser like me? I polled some friends and family, and these are the feelings that sunsets evoke for them:

> peaceful
> relaxed
> comforted
> happy
> calm
> reflective
> nostalgic
> hopeful
> content
> that God is bigger than everything
> that God is in control
> that God loves us
> a longing for loved ones passed away
> a longing for home

After earnestly seeking God's face… Every. Single. Day.

Bad things still happen. We make poor choices. We make mistakes. Our loved ones make bad choices, bad decisions.

But God allows things to happen in order to change our path for our best, IF we listen to him. He does give us free will after all.

But who knew that God could take our scraps and turn them into gold?

In all of this, where is the peace that passes all understanding?

I have prayed for years. I can honestly remember being a little girl and writing out my prayers to God. I've always believed in prayer. And I've believed in the power of God through prayer. I prayed earnestly all throughout my mom's battle with cancer, and I continued my desperate prayers following her going home to heaven.

It was a little while later that I began to struggle in my prayer life. I believe God has a plan because his Word says so, "For I know the plans I have for you…," and I believe he desires good for his children.

So…why pray? If God has a plan, what are my prayers for? Am I supposed to pray for healing knowing that the healing may be on this earth or the healing may not happen until heaven? We're instructed to pray for God's will be done. Am I supposed to pray for anything else?

With all my questions laid bare, I delved into the Scripture and into prayer.

Turns out, prayer isn't about me…(I know, right? Shocking.)

Prayer is ALL about God.

Prayer is OUR relationship WITH God.

Ephesians 6:11–20 implores us to put on the whole armor of God and then to "pray always, with all prayers and supplication in the Spirit."

So while we're out chasing sunsets, we should be vigilant to chase after God through prayer.

Prayer is where battles are fought and won.

Prayer is our warfare.

Prayer is where we find peace.

Day 1

There are lots of prayers and lots of people who prayed throughout the Bible.

God gives us instructions.

The Lord's prayer.

Jesus spoke to his disciples and a crowd one day.

> This, then, is how you should pray: "Our Father in heaven, hallowed be your name, your kingdom come, your will be done, on earth as it is in heaven. Give us today our daily bread. And forgive us our debts as we also have forgiven our debtors. And lead us not into temptation but deliver us from the evil one." (Matthew 6:9–13)

"Our Father in heaven, hallowed be your name."

Today, pray to the Father in heaven and praise him. Hallowed is he. Thank him today for his creation and for his majesty. Praise and honor him in prayer for his omnipotence, omnipresence, and omniscience. He is our all-powerful God. He is our Abba, Father.

Day 2

This, then, is how you should pray: "Our Father in heaven, hallowed be your name, your kingdom come, your will be done, on earth as it is in heaven. Give us today our daily bread. And forgive us our debts as we also have forgiven our debtors. And lead us not into temptation, but deliver us from the evil one."

—Matthew 6:9–13

"Your kingdom come."

Pray for the kingdom of heaven. Pray today and ask God to use you for his kingdom. Ask God to use you to ADD believers to his kingdom.

Be still.
Listen for his voice.
Be still.
Allow God to speak to you.
Be still.
Sense the Holy Spirit.
Pray for Yahweh's kingdom to come.

Day 3

This, then, is how you should pray: "Our Father in heaven, hallowed be your name, your kingdom come, your will be done, on earth as it is in heaven. Give us today our daily bread. And forgive us our debts as we also have forgiven our debtors. And lead us not into temptation, but deliver us from the evil one."

—Matthew 6:9–13

"Your will be done."

This can be so difficult, right? We're human. We're intelligent. We know what's good for us. And we think we know what's good for others too. Am I right?

God's will.

His plan for us.

His good and perfect will.

This can be hard, especially depending on our circumstances or situation. But our Father in heaven wants what is best for us. His will is what is best for us and for his kingdom.

We don't normally pray for God's will in situations that are already good or pleasing or easy. We pray for God's will in difficult and trying situations.

Today, make your requests be known to the Father, then pray for his will to be done.

Pause and listen for his voice. Sense the presence of the Holy Spirit.

Pray again.

Let God know you are pouring your heart out to him. Pray again to the Father, "Your will be done."

Be quiet.

His will is good.
His will can be hard.
Just ask Jesus.

Day 4

This, then, is how you should pray: "Our Father in heaven, hallowed be your name, your kingdom come, your will be done, on earth as it is in heaven. Give us today our daily bread. And forgive us our debts as we also have forgiven our debtors. And lead us not into temptation, but deliver us from the evil one."

—Matthew 6:9–13

"Give is today our daily bread."

Thank God today for your food. Thank him for the nourishment that he provides. Thank him for clean water to drink. Thank him for your garden if you have one. Thank him for the grocery store and the abundance there.

Ask God to help you make healthy choices for your nourishment. Ask God to guide you to foods that are good for you. Ask God to guide you to choose drinks that make you a healthier, better person for his service and an honest steward of the foods that you have access to.

Ask God to reveal to you how you might be able to help others that do not have access to food or money for food for their family.

Ask God to speak to you if food or drink is a stumbling block for you. The Holy Spirit can speak to you. Keep your heart and mind open to hear.

Now thank God for Jesus, the Bread of Life. Bless us today with our portion.

Day 5

This, then, is how you should pray: "Our Father in heaven, hallowed be your name, your kingdom come, your will be done, on earth as it is in heaven. Give us today our daily bread. And forgive us our debts as we also have forgiven our debtors. And lead us not into temptation, but deliver us from the evil one."

—Matthew 6:9–13

"And forgive us our debts."

Wow! Another hard part.

Forgive us, Lord, where we fail. My oh my, what a laundry list this is.

Forgive us for the things we say that we shouldn't. Forgive us for the things we don't say that we should. Forgive us because we are stingy and greedy and afraid. Forgive us for the thoughts we think that hurt you. Forgive us for our jealousy, our gluttony, or our covetousness. Forgive us for our laziness. Forgive us for our lack of participation in your church. Forgive us for our pride; we think we are so smart. Forgive us for our poor choices, since we are so intelligent and we think we know what's best for us. Forgive us for ignoring your voice, your heeding. Forgive our unbelief. Forgive us for not loving people like we should. Forgive us for not using our talents for you. Forgive us for not using our spiritual gifts like you have called us to.

Why do we put so many things ahead of you? Forgive us for not putting you first.

Father, there are so many things to ask forgiveness for. We fail you so much, but you love us still.

God, we ask you to help us be better.

Every day. Every minute.

Day 6

This, then, is how you should pray: "Our Father in heaven, hallowed be your name, your kingdom come, your will be done, on earth as it is in heaven. Give us today our daily bread. And forgive us our debts as we also have forgiven our debtors. And lead us not into temptation, but deliver us from the evil one."

—Matthew 6:9–13

"As we also have forgiven our debtors"

We thought this prayer thing might be difficult but it just became almost impossible. That's how it feels, right?

Forgiveness.

Such a messy word.

We have so many excuses.

Forgiveness isn't about us saying "It's okay." Forgiveness isn't even about someone acknowledging the hurt they caused.

There are times in our lives that someone can step in and wreak havoc, and they may never know what absolute hurt and heartbreak they caused you.

Those words spoken can bounce around in your head and make your heart race.

Forgiveness is giving your hurt to God and asking him to please change and heal your spirit.

Protect yourself. Don't put yourself or keep yourself in a bad or abusive situation.

But ask God to help you give the bitterness and anger of unforgiveness over to him. Hand it over to him.

Pray diligently.

Releasing the unforgiveness and the emotions and feelings that accompany it doesn't happen overnight.

Try not to let unforgiveness furnish an apartment in your heart and mind. You need to evict that. If unforgiveness tries to move in, don't feed and water him. Unforgiveness will get hungry and thirsty, and he'll leave. Let God escort him out.

Day 7

This, then, is how you should pray: "Our Father in heaven, hallowed be your name, your kingdom come, your will be done, on earth as it is in heaven. Give us today our daily bread. And forgive us our debts as we also have forgiven our debtors. And lead us not into temptation, but deliver us from the evil one."

—Matthew 6:9–13

"And lead us not into temptation."

Thankfully, today's prayer might be a bit easier than the past two days.

God, please keep us from temptation.

We know God will not tempt us, but he does allow us to be tempted. We also know from where the temptation comes…the evil one.

The devil enjoys tempting us, especially if we are praying often or learning to pray. The devil hates for us to be closer to God and in fellowship with him, and he will really stop at nothing to get us to put God on the back burner.

If God is not a priority in our life, the devil doesn't have anything to worry about, really.

The devil is very afraid when we are in fellowship with God and are doing work for God.

Be aware of the wiles of the devil. Ask God to help you be aware of temptations. The devil is like a roaring lion roaming around looking to devour us.

Be aware that temptation doesn't typically come up and smack you in the face. The devil is sneaky.

Take note of your thoughts first. There's a battlefield in our minds.

Take note of what you are seeing, then take note of your thoughts.

Take note of what you hear, then take note of your thoughts again.

Ask God to help you be aware of temptation and take your thoughts captive to the Lord.

Day 8

This, then, is how you should pray: "Our Father in heaven, hallowed be your name, your kingdom come, your will be done, on earth as it is in heaven. Give us today our daily bread. And forgive us our debts as we also have forgiven our debtors. And lead us not into temptation, but deliver us from the evil one."

—Matthew 6:9–13

"But deliver us from the evil one."

I'm fairly certain we have no real idea just how much power is in the name of Jesus.

Maybe you have been in a position when you have called out audibly for Jesus, and after your experience, you know firsthand, *for real* for real, just how much power is in his name.

I had a very good friend in college, and she had such an experience.

She had fallen into temptation (like yesterday's Scripture spoke about), which also means she had fallen into a trap, a bad situation.

She had made attempts to remedy the situation, but the devil is persistent.

One night, very late, the drunken devil came knocking on her apartment door. The knocking didn't wake her initially, but then the POUNDING on the door did. She lay quietly in the bed, afraid, hoping the devil would retreat. He did not. He began to yell.

She was concerned that her neighbors would be disturbed by the pounding, yelling devil, so she tiptoed to open the apartment door.

The devil rushed in. He was drunk, and he was mad. He shoved her up against the wall of her living room with his hand on her throat.

She could see his angry, evil face in the streetlight flooding through the front window. He yelled at her and called her terrible names. He told her what a bad person she was.

Although she had made poor choices and had gotten herself into a bad situation, she knew on whom to call on to be saved.

She stayed strong.

She told the devil to leave IN THE NAME OF JESUS!

Demons flee at the mention of his name!

The devil left that night.

And he did not come back.

Day 9

David prayed, "Vindicate me, my God, and plead my cause against an unfaithful nation. Rescue me from those who are deceitful and wicked" (Psalm 43:1).

Deceit.

Deception.

Distortion of truth.

Fraud.

Trick.

We are so easily deceived.

Pray today to be filled with the spirit and to not fall for the tricks of Satan, evil, and the world. Pray for discernment, to be able to sense and know what is true and what is false. What is godly and what is wicked. Pray to have excellent recall of the Scripture. Don't let the world tell you what is true and what is just.

The devil "walks about like a roaring lion, seeking whom he may devour" (1 Peter 5:8b NKJV).

The devil hates God's creation. He hates God's people.

Do not be deceived by his tricks and schemes.

Pray to not be deceived.

Day 10

The Armor of God

Finally, be strong in the Lord and in his mighty power. Put on the full armor of God, so that you can take your stand against the devil's schemes. For our struggle is not against flesh and blood, but against the rulers, against the authorities, against the powers of this dark world and against the spiritual forces of evil in the heavenly realms. Therefore, put on the full armor of God, so that when the day of evil comes, you may be able to stand your ground, and after you have done everything, to stand. Stand firm then, with the belt of truth buckled around your waist, with the breastplate of righteousness in place, and with your feet fitted with the readiness that comes from the gospel of peace. In addition to all this, take up the shield of faith, with which you can extinguish all the flaming arrows of the evil one. Take the helmet of salvation and the sword of the Spirit, which is the word of God.

And pray in the Spirit on all occasions with all kinds of prayers and requests. With this in mind, be alert and always keep on praying for all the Lord's people. (Ephesians 6:10–18)

Today, pray to be strong in the Lord and in his mighty power. Call upon his strength today—power and strength to stand against the devil's schemes.

Day 11

T oday, pray to have the belt of truth buckled around your waist.

What is truth?

Jesus is the way, the truth, and the life. God's Word is truth.

Pray for these things to be ever present in your heart and life. Pray to have your belt on straight and not shifting.

Like with so many things in our lives, this can be challenging. We are bombarded with disappointments, lies, unmet expectations, and broken dreams.

Remember the truth. Study the truth. Ruminate on the truth.

Pray to have the belt of truth buckled straight and snugly around your waist. Unshifting, unwavering truth.

Day 12

Today, pray to have the breastplate of righteousness secured in place.

Righteousness comes from Jesus Christ alone. We are not perfect, but we are to seek to become righteous. To daily pray for righteousness, to seek to be more like Christ every day, to study the Scripture and desire to live out God's plan for our lives. Pray to have the breastplate of righteousness secured in order to avoid and resist temptation, to flee from sin that ensnares us, and to protect our hearts from Satan's attempts to trap us.

Day 13

Today, pray to have your feet fitted with the readiness that comes from the gospel of peace.

The gospel is the good news of Jesus Christ, our Savior. It is peace. We find our peace in the pages of the Gospel. We find peace over fear and worry. We place the gospel of peace on our feet in order to walk the Christian journey.

Roman soldiers' shoes had small spikes on the soles for stability in marching over rough terrain and for better positioning of their feet during battle. Those spikes helped them stand their ground.

Pray today to have your feet shod with the readiness that comes from the gospel of peace, so we can share peace with a sin-sick and dying world; we can share the good news of Jesus Christ our Savior.

Day 14

"Take up the shield of faith, with which you can extinguish all the flaming arrows of the evil one."

Today, pray to be strong in your faith. Faith in the Father, the Son, and the Holy Spirit is our foundation. With our faith, we will be strong enough to dodge the flaming arrows—the lies that we are told on a daily basis, the negative thoughts that we have, and the past that returns to haunt us. All of these can catch us off guard and surprise us at times.

Pray to be strong in your belief and faith that God is who he says he is and that you are who he says you are. Pray and ask God to increase your faith in him and in his Word. We have the tools to stop the fiery darts. We must choose to take up our shield.

Day 15

"Take the helmet of salvation."

Salvation is accepting Jesus Christ as our Savior and asking the Holy Spirit to dwell in us. With salvation, we receive the gift of eternal life, wherein upon our physical death on this earth, our souls live on in eternity in heaven with the Trinity.

We must be saved in order to put on our helmet.

Why a helmet? Because the battle is in our mind. What thoughts do you think? What do you ruminate on in your mind?

Pray today to have your helmet of salvation securely on your head. Your helmet will protect your mind from the blows that the devil will deliver. The helmet will help you to have a clear vision of the path that you are walking.

Pray and thank God for sending his one and only son, Jesus, to die on the cross for us. Pray and thank God for the gift of salvation. Have some quiet time to hear from God. He loves you, and he desires to speak to you. Thank him and listen for his voice.

Day 16

"And the sword of the Spirit, which is the word of God."

The Holy Bible. God inspired. God breathed. Infallible. True. Inerrant.

This sword is not only our defensive weapon but also our offensive weapon.

We must study the Word of God and hide the Word of God in our hearts. We have God's holy Word to defend us against the wiles of the devil and to strengthen us offensively.

Pray today and thank God for blessing us with his Word. Pray and ask God for discernment as you read through the Scripture today, that he would bring understanding and not confusion. Pray and ask God to help you store his Word in your heart.

Day 17

And pray in the Spirit on all occasions with
all kinds of prayers and requests
—Ephesians 6:18

Paul wrote this, and he is asking God's people to pray in the Spirit on ALL occasions with ALL kinds of prayers and requests.

This makes me so, so excited! God wants us to pray. He desires that we pray and fellowship with him. He desires the communication with us. He longs for us to slow down and spend time with him. He wants to hear our desires and our burdens.

This is what this book is about—PRAYER.

Pray today and thank God for prayer. Thank him that Jesus made a way for us to pray and confess our sin directly to the Father in Jesus's name. We have direct access to the Creator of the universe. We have direct access to Yahweh, the one true God. Pray today and thank God for hearing each of our prayers. Pray to hear his voice today. What will God speak to you today as you thank him for prayer and for hearing us each time we pray?

Day 18

With this in mind, be alert and always keep
on praying for all the Lord's people.

—Ephesians 6:18

God desires that we pray for one another and lift one another to his throne of grace.

Today, pray for the Church, the body of Christ joined together. Christ's bride. Christians and believers in Christ are persecuted daily in our world. Saul, before his salvation and name change to Paul, was a vigilant persecutor of Christians. Many Christians still face persecution today.

Keep your eyes open to the treatment of believers everywhere. Stay strong in your faith and be vigilant in prayer.

Day 19

Pray also for me, that whenever I speak, words may be
given me so that I will fearlessly make known the mystery
of the gospel, for which I am an ambassador in chains.
—Ephesians 6:19–20a

Paul was requesting prayer to have the words to speak. We should
do the same. We may not be pastors, church leaders, Bible teachers,
or foreign missionaries, but shouldn't we also ask for God to give us
the words to speak so that we, too, can make known the mystery of
the gospel? What is more important than that?

Today, pray and ask that God would give you the words to share
the gospel. Pray to have "your conversation be always full of grace,
seasoned with salt, so that you may know how to answer everyone"
(Colossians 4:6).

Day 20

Pray that I may declare it fearlessly as I should.

—Ephesians 6:20b

Fearless.

Without fear.

Today, pray to not be afraid. If fear is a struggle for you, pray to hand that over to the Father today. Confess your fear. Let God have it. Pray to declare the gospel without fear or shame. Pray and ask God to use you for his purpose and to serve him without fear. Pray and ask God to show you where fear might be holding you back.

Spend some quiet time listening for the Lord's voice. If you ask him to reveal where fear is in the forefront, spend a few moments listening for his response.

Are there things that you know God has been calling you to do in his name? Are there jobs or opportunities to serve that God has placed on your heart but you have been afraid to step out and follow through, or you have made excuses that are based off of fear? Hand those over to the Lord and ask him to remove the fear.

Pray and ask God to make you fearless.

Day 21

M oses prayed.

But Moses sought the favor of the Lord, his God. "Lord, he said, 'why should your anger burn against your people, whom you brought out of Egypt with great power and a mighty hand? Why should the Egyptians say, 'It was with evil intent that he brought them out, to kill them in the mountains and to wipe them off the face of the earth? Turn from your fierce anger, relent and do not bring disaster on your people. Remember your servants Abraham, Isaac and Israel, to whom you swore by your own self. I will make your descendants as numerous as the stars in the sky and I will give your descendants all this land I promised them, and it will be their inheritance forever. Then the Lord relented and did not bring on his people the disaster he had threatened" (Exodus 32:11–14).

Moses prayed, and we should not be afraid to pray. We should not think that God doesn't want to hear what we have to say. The things that concern us are important to him.

Moses sought the Lord, his God, in prayer. God heard Moses and relented and did not bring the disaster to his people that he had threatened.

We most certainly can feel threatened at times today, can't we?

Today, pray about the things that you feel threatened by. God hears our prayers. Your fervent prayers could cause him to relent.

You won't know unless you pray.

Day 22

On the day the Lord gave the Amorites over to Israel,
Joshua said to the Lord in the presence of Israel:
'Sun stand still over Gibeon, and you,
moon, over the Valley of Aijalon.'
So the sun stood still, and the moon stopped, till
the nation avenged itself on its enemies,
as it is written in the book of Jashar.
The sun stopped in the middle of the sky and delayed
going down about a full day. There has never been a day
like it before or since, a day when the Lord listened to a
human being. Surely the Lord was fighting for Israel.

—Joshua 10:12–14

And He will fight for you today.

We may not be praying for the sun to stay high in the sky and for the moon to stop moving, but our sincere prayers for our families, our friends, our nation, and our world are as important to God today as Joshua's prayer was then. When we are praying for God's will to be done and when we pray for his kingdom, he hears us. Find peace in knowing that he hears our prayers, then listen for his voice. What is he telling you today? Do you need the sun to stay high in the sky a little longer? Ask him today.

Day 23

Then Jonah prayed to the Lord his God from the belly of the fish, saying, "I called out to the Lord, out of my distress, and he answered me; out of the belly of Sheol I cried, and you heard my voice. For you cast me into the deep, into the heart of the seas, and the flood surrounded me; all your waves and your billows passed over me. Then I said, 'I am driven away from your sight; yet I shall again look upon your holy temple.' The waters closed in over me to take my life; the deep surrounded me; weeds were wrapped about my head at the roots of the mountains. I went down to the land whose bars closed upon me forever; yet you brought up my life from the pit, O Lord my God. When my life was fainting away, I remembered the Lord, and my prayer came to you, into your holy temple. Those who pay regard to vain idols forsake their hope of steadfast love. But I with the voice of thanksgiving will sacrifice to you; what I have vowed I will pay. Salvation belongs to the Lord! And the Lord spoke to the fish, and it vomited Jonah out upon the dry land"

—Jonah 2:1–10 (ESV)

Are you feeling like you're in the belly of a fish today? I can't really imagine that, but I do imagine that it would be very stinky, sticky, dark, and wet. And I would probably feel very trapped.

If you're feeling like that today, pray like Jonah and ask the Lord for help.

Jonah had been running away from the Lord. He had been afraid; then, he found himself trapped.

From the belly of Sheol, cry out to God today. Maybe you're not trapped, but you know someone who is. Pray for them. Be their prayer warrior and intervene on their behalf today.

God can still cause fish to vomit.

Day 24

But encourage one another daily, as long as it is called 'Today,'
so that none of you may be hardened by sin's deceitfulness.

—Hebrews 3:13

Pray today to not be deceived by sin and, therefore, hardened by sin. Pray the same also for your family. Pray that you would be aware of the devil's tactics today. Be sure to put on the full armor of God. Pray for encouragement for yourself and those you love.

Pray this while it is still called *today*. Don't put off praying.

Your prayers wage war on sin.

Believe it.

Day 25

Three times I pleaded with the Lord to take it away from me. But he said to me, "My grace is sufficient for you, for my power is made perfect in weakness." Therefore I will boast all the more gladly about my weaknesses, so that Christ's power may rest on me.

—2 Corinthians 12:8–9

Paul prayed and pleaded with God to remove the thorn from him. We can too. God hears our prayers. He hears our pleas. Like with Paul, God's plan may not be to remove our thorn. Paul came to accept his thorn and to even appreciate the thorn. He considered it a weakness, and that weakness caused him to rely more on God. Paul came to boast about his weaknesses because he could sense God's power resting on him through the weakness.

So, yes, we should pray and plead to God, but most importantly we should sense God, sense the Holy Spirit, feel God working in us and through us, all for his good pleasure.

Day 26

And will not God bring about justice for his chosen ones, who cry out to him day and night? Will he keep putting them off? I tell you, he will see that they get justice, and quickly. However, when the Son of Man comes, will he find faith on the earth?

—Luke 18:7–8

Jesus taught a parable about a widow who pleaded consistently to a judge.

The same applies to us today.

Jesus is encouraging us to plead consistently day and night. He will bring about justice for us. He will protect us from our adversaries. We are to seek him continually, day after day, night after night, season after season, and year after year.

He desires that we seek his face, be diligent, consistent, follow his statutes, and seek his will and not our own. Stay in relationship with him. Consistently.

Day 27

Therefore, my dear friends, as you have always obeyed-not only
in my presence, but now much more in my absence-continue to
work out your salvation with fear and trembling, for it is God who
works in you to will and to act in order to fulfill his good purpose.
—Philippians 2:12–13

God's purpose. God's plan.

It is good. He is good.

Pray today to fulfill God's purposes. He has made each of us for
a purpose, each with different gifts, to carry out his will.

Our greatest hope is not to change God's plan, but instead to
pray and bring about his good purpose.

Day 28

Then you will call on me and come and pray
to me, and I will listen to you.

—Jeremiah 29:12

God is inviting us to call on him, pray to him…and he will listen. His Word says so. God desires that we fellowship and have relationship with him. He created us for his pleasure. He delights in us and delights in conversation with us.

Spend time in prayer today just allowing God to place upon your heart exactly whom or what to pray about. He will place on your heart and mind the prayer. Listen closely.

Day 29

Therefore, confess your sins to one another, and pray for one another so that you may be healed. A prayer of a righteous person, when it is brought about, can accomplish much.

—James 5:16 (NASB)

God says our prayers matter; they can accomplish much. Our prayers work because we ask. We always must ask according to God's will, but God desires that we seek him and make our requests known to him.

Today…confess and ask. Then, listen closely.

Day 30

Rejoice always, pray continually, give thanks in all circumstances; for this is God's will for you in Christ Jesus.
— 1 Thessalonians 5:16–18

Rejoice.
Pray continually.
Give thanks in all circumstances.
Do this.
We can do these things constantly. Be ever in prayer. Pray when you are grocery shopping. Rejoice when you are driving. Pray while you are riding the bus. Rejoice while you are cooking. Pray while you are walking. Rejoice while you are cleaning.
Lift your praises and prayers to the Most High continually.

Day 31

Continue earnestly in prayer, being vigilant in it with thanksgiving.
—Colossians 4:2 (NKJV)

Paul is imploring the people of Colossae to continue earnestly in prayer, to be vigilant in it, and be with thanksgiving.

There are so many verses and so much Scripture is written asking, imploring Christ's followers to pray, be vigilant in prayer, and make our petitions known to God. Do we just read over these words? Do we ignore them? Do we consider prayer to be unimportant, that it doesn't matter, that it does no good? Do we think prayer is a waste of time? Is prayer too time consuming?

Probably all of these to some degree. And we couldn't be more wrong. I think that's exactly what the devil wants us to think and feel. Why? Because prayer is our direct relationship to God. Of course, the devil wants us to repeat written prayers and to feel like our Heavenly Father is too far and too big and just too unreachable. But we know the devil is a liar and the father of lies and deception.

Prayer is a big deal.

Prayer is our direct conversation with God. Like I said before, it's the root of our relationship with our Creator. If prayer wasn't such a big deal, God would not have mentioned it so much in his Word.

Prayer is a big deal, and we are asked to be vigilant in it.

Day 32

For the eyes of the Lord are on the righteous and
his ears are attentive to their prayer, but the face
of the Lord is against those who do evil.

—1 Peter 3:12

God's Word says that his ears are attentive to our prayers. Wow!
The Creator of the universe HEARS MY PRAYERS! I am so humbled by
this. Who am I? I often feel really, really small and fairly unimportant, but THE LORD'S EARS ARE ATTENTIVE TO MY PRAYERS!

He hears. He cares.

He has a plan for us. He desires to have relationship with us.
Pray…

Day 33

Ask and it will be given to you; seek and you will find;
knock and the door will be opened to you. For everyone
who asks receives; the one who seeks finds; and to
the one who knocks, the door will be opened.

—Matthew 7:7–8

Ask.

Ask is another word for pray.

Seek, and you will find.

We get really confused in our world today about asking and receiving and seeking and finding. We get caught up in material things and possessions, thinking that receiving material things are our blessings.

In reality, receiving more of Jesus is the real blessing, knowing him more.

Prayer is relationship. Ask about your relationship. Ask regarding the desires of your heart. Ask regarding God's plan for you. As Christians, we are to worship God and seek to make Jesus known as the Savior—the way, the truth, and the life. Seek to know God's path for you, so that you can carry out that plan and give the glory and praise to God.

That is what the "ask, seek, and knock" is leading us to more of God.

Day 34

Let us therefore come boldly to the throne of grace, that we
may obtain mercy and find grace to help in time of need.
—Hebrews 4:16 (NKJV)

Again...wow! Just wow! God is so good to us. We are filthy, but
he loves us. And when we are saved by grace through faith in Jesus
Christ, he calls us his own.

And in Hebrews, it says, we find mercy and grace to help in
time of need. I don't know about you, but it seems like I am in a
constant state of need. I am always seeking help from the Lord. And
in our world today, we surely are thirsty for mercy and grace. So what
to do? Hebrews says to come boldly to the throne of grace. That
is approaching God through prayer, entering into conversation and
deep relationship with him. Maybe you are a super fortunate soul
that has avoided "a time of need." If you live long enough, your time
will come. This "need," is when you need strength that is more than
you possess; you need peace that passes understanding; you need
power to carry on; you need grief to be replaced with joy. When we
go boldly to the throne of grace, we find mercy and grace.

Approach the throne in prayer, and pray without ceasing.

Day 35

And call on me in the day of trouble; I will
deliver you, and you will honor me.

—Psalm 50:15

God WANTS us to call on him. He desires that we call on him in our day of trouble. Then, even more than we deserve, he says in his Word, he will deliver you. Deliver you, me, us out of our trouble when we call upon him. And then, we must give him all the glory.

Maybe you're not experiencing any trouble at the moment. Everything is coming up roses for you, and that would be so wonderful. But I think you probably know someone that is in trouble. The world is full of trouble and turmoil.

Today, pray and talk with God about your trouble. He already knows, but he loves conversation with us. And if you have no trouble, definitely thank him for the peace you have now, then lift up to the throne of grace the people and situations that are embroiled in all kinds of trouble.

Thank God again today that he asks us to call on him in our day of trouble. I'm so thankful we have a God that cares so deeply for us.

Day 36

Be joyful in hope, patient in affliction, faithful in prayer.
—Romans 12:12

Paul wrote for us to be joyful because we have hope, to be patient in affliction, and aren't we experiencing affliction every day? We must be patient. Then, Paul asks us to be faithful in prayer. If prayer didn't matter, Paul wouldn't talk about it. But Paul tells us to be faithful in prayer.

Faithful: to be loyal, constant, and steadfast. So Paul is asking us to be loyal in prayer, to be constant in prayer, and to be steadfast in prayer. Paul knew that prayer is our relationship with the Savior. Paul knew that prayer changes us and changes our hearts. Paul wanted the church to know just how important prayer is.

Today, thank God for his faithfulness to his people and thank him for prayer. Thank him that we have access to him, our Father in heaven, through prayer.

Then remain faithful in it.

Day 37

Do not be anxious about anything, but in every situation, by prayer and petition, with thanksgiving, present your requests to God.

—Philippians 4:6

Paul. The greatest missionary. He knew of trouble. He also knew of the life-changing grace of God. Paul tells us again to not be anxious but to present our requests to God with thanksgiving—always with thanksgiving and awe, that the Creator of the universe cares to hear of our cries and troubles. And Paul says in every situation, by prayer and petition.

Today, do not be anxious. We all have a decent amount of anxiety in the world. In our own lives personally and in the whole world, so many things bring us anxiety. But our God has the whole world in his hands, and he cares for us. When we seek his face and yearn to complete his will in us; when we pray and long to get to know him more, he will hear our cries and petitions and will send his peace. We must be faithful in prayer and in presenting our petitions to him.

Then be still, be quiet, and listen for what God would speak to you.

Day 38

For this reason, since the day we heard about you, we
have not stopped praying for you. We continually ask
God to fill you with the knowledge of his will through all
the wisdom and understanding that the Spirit gives
—Colossians 1:9

Again, Paul is praying. Paul knew prayer was the key to under-standing the Father and the Father's will. Paul says we have not stopped praying for you.

Are there people or situations in our own lives that we have stopped praying for or about? We get tired; we become annoyed at our own repetitiveness. We think surely God would have handled this by now. We think things could never change after all this time. We may even think that God is bored with our same old requests.

He's not.

We need to be like Paul and not stop praying. Maybe we need to change our prayer, change our request, and change our words; but know that God hears, and he never stops working. He doesn't give up on us or throw in the towel. His desire is for us to know him and to know the saving power of his son Jesus.

Pray today for the strength to continue praying. Ask God to renew your spirit and to help you continue in your prayers.

Day 39

Watch and pray so that you will not fall into temptation.
The spirit is willing, but the flesh is weak.

—Matthew 26:41

Jesus was speaking to his disciples, but he was also speaking to us. "Watch and pray," he said.

Watch and pray so you do not fall into temptation. We know our spirit is willing, but our flesh is so weak. We need strength to pray. We need God's strength passed on to us to have the strength to pray and not fall.

Also, Jesus was fully aware of the need for prayer and just how important prayer was—so important that he asked the disciples to pray. If there had been another way, Jesus would have given them different instructions. He would have made another request.

But Jesus asked his closest followers to pray in the garden with him.

How much more should we pray and treasure prayer?

Day 40

Going a little farther, he fell with his face to the ground
and prayed, "My Father, if it is possible, may this cup be
taken from me. Yet not as I will, but as you will."

—Matthew 26:39

Jesus prayed.

We should pray.

If Jesus, the son of God, prays in the garden, how much more should we pray...

Jesus knew the plan. He knew why he had come. He accepted the plan, but it was painful. Even Jesus prayed to God the Father. He communicated his desires and longings. He knew what was to come, and still he prayed for another way. Jesus knew the Father; he and the father are one, yet Jesus STILL prayed.

We must seek God in prayer, continually and on all occasions— to speak with him, to make our petitions known to him, to thank him, to worship him, to get to know him, and to know his heart.

If Jesus prayed, we should be all the more devoted to prayer. We must know the father and hear him speak to us.

Prayer is our relationship with God.

Prayer is where we find the peace that passes all understanding.

Peace I leave with you; my peace I give you. I do not give to you as the world gives. Do not let your hearts be troubled and do not be afraid.

—John 14:27

P ray and seek the peace that only comes from a deep, knowing, trusting, and understanding relationship with God—to seek to know the heart of the father and to have relationship with him.

Every minute of every day will not be peaceful. We live in a fallen world. But we can "seek first the kingdom of God and his righteousness," and we'll find the peace that passes all understanding.

Pray and seek the Prince of Peace.

Romans Road to Salvation

*S*tep *1*: Everyone needs salvation because all have sinned.

> *As the Scriptures say, "No one is righteous—not even one. No one is truly wise; no one is seeking God. All have turned away; all have become useless. No one does good, not a single one."… For everyone has sinned; we all fall short of God's glorious standard. (Romans 3:10–12 and 23* NLT)

Step 2: The price (or consequence) of sin is death.

> *For the wages of sin is death, but the free gift of God is eternal life through Christ Jesus our Lord. (Romans 6:23* NLT)

Step 3: Jesus Christ died for our sins. He paid the price for our death.

> *But God showed his great love for us by sending Christ to die for us while we were still sinners. (Romans 5:8* NLT).

Step 4: We receive salvation and *eternal life* through faith in Jesus Christ.

> *If you confess with your mouth that Jesus is Lord and believe in your heart that God raised him from the dead, you will be saved. For it is by believing in your heart that you are made right with God,*

and it is by confessing with your mouth that you are saved... For "Everyone who calls on the name of the Lord will be saved." (Romans 10:9–10 and 13 NLT).

Step 5: Salvation through Jesus Christ brings us into a relationship of peace with God.

> *Therefore, since we have been made right in God's sight by faith, we have peace with God because of what Jesus Christ our Lord has done for us.* (Romans 5:1 NLT)

> *So now there is no condemnation for those who belong to Christ Jesus.* (Romans 8:1 NLT)

> *And I am convinced that nothing can ever separate us from God's love. Neither death nor life, neither angels nor demons, neither our fears for today nor our worries about tomorrow—not even the powers of hell can separate us from God's love. No power in the sky above or in the earth below— indeed, nothing in all creation will ever be able to separate us from the love of God that is revealed in Christ Jesus our Lord.* (Romans 8:38–39 NLT)

Responding to the Romans Road

If you believe the Romans Road leads to the path of truth, you can respond by receiving God's free gift of salvation today. Here's how to take your personal journey down the Romans Road:

1. Admit you are a sinner.
2. Understand that as a sinner, you deserve death.
3. Believe Jesus Christ died on the *cross* to save you from *sin* and death.
4. Repent by turning from your old life of sin to a *new life* in Christ.
5. Receive, through faith in Jesus Christ, his free gift of salvation.

About the Author

Shannon lives in Tennessee with her husband and is momma to two wonderful sons. She enjoys spending time with her family, reading, writing, weight training, everything football, beaches, summer, traveling, and sunsets. Shannon is also the author of Gather Yourself: My Early Journey Through Grief.

CPSIA information can be obtained
at www.ICGtesting.com
Printed in the USA
BVHW081100151121
621687BV00004B/107

9 781638 141419